MATERIALS

What is stuff made from?

Emily Kington

Stone is a hard and heavy material. Probably too heavy for this ant to carry.

CONTENTS

Words that appear in **bold** are explained in the glossary.

The answers to the questions are on pages 20–21.

www.hungrytomato.com

WHAT ARE MATERIALS?

Materials are what things are made of. We use different materials to make different objects.

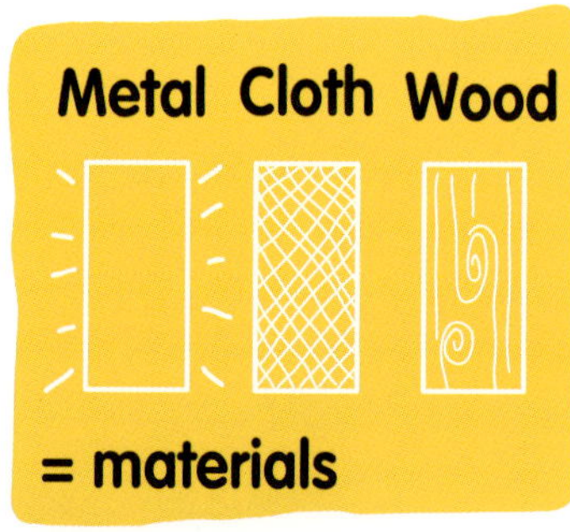

Metal, wood, paper, glass, plastic, and cloth are some of the materials that we use every day.

Some objects are made of just one material.

Other objects are made of two or more different materials.

Metal, cloth, and wood are materials.

Stickmen's Challenge Now it's your turn . . .

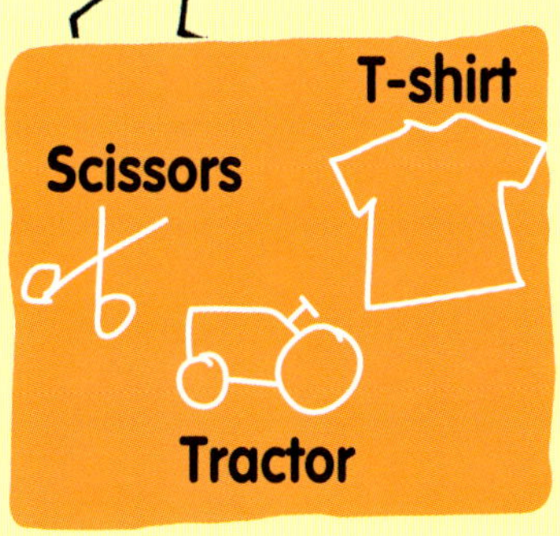

Look at the scissors, the T-shirt, and the tractor. Are these objects or materials?

STONE

Stone is a hard, heavy **natural** material. It is the same material as the rocks that make mountains and cliffs.

Stone = heavy and long-lasting

Stone is found underground or on cliffs and mountains.

Stone lasts a long time. Many buildings are made from stone.

Stone does not bend, but it can be cut into shapes or broken into pieces.

This huge stone statue is on an island in the Pacific ocean.

Stickmen's Challenge
Now it's your turn . . .

If you step in a patch of soft mud you will leave a footprint. What happens if you step on a block of stone?

METAL

Metal is a material made from some kinds of stone. The stone is smashed into powder. Then it is heated so the metal comes out of the stone.

Stone that contains metal is called ore. This is iron ore.

Metals are hard like stone, but they can bend.

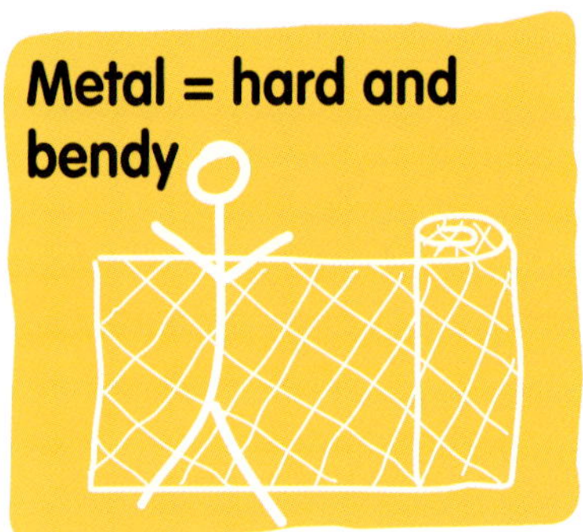

Metal is a good material for making things like bendy fence wire.

Metals are strong and difficult to break. They usually look shiny.

Stickmen's Challenge Now it's your turn . . .

What will be left?

Look at all the different objects below. What will be left if you take all the metal objects away?

WOOD

Wood is a natural material. It comes from trees that have been cut down.

Inside a tree trunk there are rings. A new ring grows each year.

The rings make a pattern in wood that is called grain.

If you count the rings, you can find out the age of the tree.

Metal saw = can cut wood

Wood is a hard material, but it is not as hard as stone or metal. Wood can easily be cut and shaped with metal tools.

Wooden flute

Wooden chess pieces

Stickmen's Challenge Now it's your turn . . .

Wooden saw

You can cut wood with a metal saw. Can you cut metal with a wooden saw?

PAPER

Paper is a soft, **artificial** material that is made from wood.

The wood is shredded into tiny pieces and soaked in water to make a mushy mixture called **pulp**. The pulp is then flattened into thin sheets and dried.

Pulp

Sheets of paper are lightweight and very easy to bend and fold. You can make paper dinorasurs out of them.

You can make a chair from pieces of wood or from strong cardboard.

Stickmen's Challenge

Now it's your turn . . .

This chair has been made from pieces of paper. What do you think will happen if you sit on it?

GLASS

Glass is a hard, artificial material that is made from sand. The sand is heated until it is very, very hot. Then it melts and turns into glass.

Hot glass is soft. It can be made into different shapes before it cools down and becomes hard.

Glass is **transparent**. This means that light passes through it.

Glass windows let light in and allow us to see out.

Stickmen's Challenge Now it's your turn . . .

You cannot see inside a metal can. Can you see inside a glass bottle?

PLASTIC

Plastic is an artificial material that is made from **crude oil**. The oil is pumped out of the ground and sent to a **refinery**.

Plastic can be made in any shape and color.

This machine is pumping oil from under the ground.

At the refinery, the oil is heated to produce plastic and other useful substances such as gasoline.

Plastic can be transparent like a bottle, hard like a plastic dinosaur, or soft like a beach ball or a duck for the bath.

Stickmen's Challenge Now it's your turn . . .

Plastic can also be transparent. Which plastic objects above can you see through?

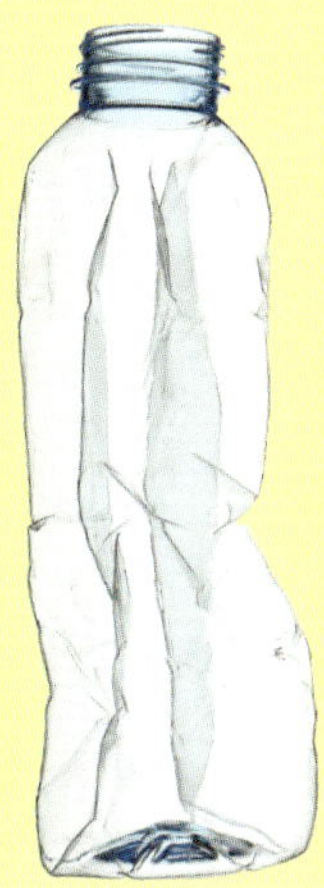

CLOTH

Cloth is a soft, artificial material made from **fibers**. Some cloth is made from plastic fibers, and some is made from natural fibers.

Wool cloth is made from natural fibers from sheep and goats.

Cotton cloth is made from the natural fibers from the cotton plant.

The fibers are spun into a continuous **yarn**. Then the yarn is woven or knitted into cloth.

The cloth becomes many things such as T-shirts, jeans, and sweaters.

Stickmen's Challenge! Now it's your turn . . .

If you fold a sheet of paper in half, it will stand on end. Can you do this with a piece of cloth?

ANSWERS

Page 5

They are all objects made from materials. The scissors are an object made of metal, the T-shirt is an object made of cloth, and the tractor is an object made of wood.

Scissors, T-shirt, and tractor = objects

Page 7

Nothing will happen! If you step on a block of stone, you will not leave a footprint because the surface of stone is much too hard.

Stone = hard

Page 9

There will be nothing left because they are all made from metal. The saucepan and screws are made from steel. The trumpet is made from brass. The rings are made from gold, and the tin can is made from aluminum.

Saucepan, tin can, trumpet, gold rings and screws = metal

Page 11

No you cannot cut metal with a wooden saw because metal is a harder material than wood.

Wooden saw = cannot cut metal

Page 13

It will collapse! Pieces of paper will fold and crumple if you put weight on them, so they are not strong enough to make a chair.

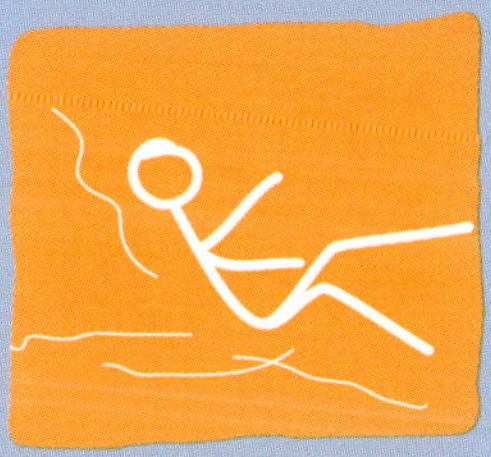

Paper chair = not strong

Page 15

Glass is a transparent material, so you can see the drink inside a glass bottle.

Glass bottle = see-through

Page 17

You can see through the bottle, the sandwich packet, and the sunglasses.

Some plastic = see-through

Page 19

You cannot make a folded piece of cloth stand on end. Cloth is so soft, it collapses under its own weight. Most paper is soft, but paper can support its own weight when it is folded.

Cloth = soft

GLOSSARY

artificial anything made by people

cloth a kind of material that is made from fibers joined together by weaving or knitting

crude oil oil that has been pumped from under the ground. It is natural and has not had anything done to it by people.

fibers thin pieces of a material, such as plastic or wool

glass a transparent material made from sand

material any substance that things are made from

metal a hard, strong material, such as gold or iron

natural anything that is made entirely by nature

paper a lightweight material made from wood

plastic an artificial material made from crude oil

pulp a material made from wood. It is wet and mushy.

refinery a place where crude oil is taken to be made into other things

stone a hard, heavy, natural material that can be dug from cliffs or mountains

transparent see-through—allows light to pass through

wood a natural material that comes from trees

yarn a long thread made of fibers twisted together

INDEX

First published in 2020 by Hungry Tomato Ltd
F1, Old Bakery Studios, Blewetts Wharf, Malpas Road, Truro, Cornwall, TR1 1QH, UK

ISBN 978 1 913077 549

Manufactured in the USA

A CIP catalog record for this book is available from the British Library.

Picture credits
SHuterstock: 1: Yaping. 2-3: djhayazaa. 4-5: 3DMAVR, Mamuka Gotsiridze, Evgeny Prokofyev, studiovin, Dzha33, Yellow Cat, onair, outc, tale, Billion Photos. 6-7: Leonard Zhukovsky, Puwadol Jaturawutthichai. 8-9: Levent Konuk, Churairat Music , Eric Isselee, Sergio Sergo, Sunshine Bunny, Ruslan Ivantsov, Boonchuay1970, Evgeny Karandaev. 10-11: Triff, Mas Hasyim , BORTEL Pavel - Pavelmidi, PhilipYb Studio, photomaster, Ewa Studio. 12-13: ConstantinosZ, v74, Hunter Bliss Images, Tatiana Popova , Victor Naumik. 14-15: Ossi, maradon 333, AlenKadr, nevodka, Pineapple studio. 16-17: catalina.m, irin-k, TheFarAwayKingdom, eNjoy iStyle, By irin-k, PJjaruwan. 18-19: Eric Isselee, Ines Behrens-Kunkel, Pencil case, Grigorita Ko, aopsan.

Every effort has been made to trace the copyright holders, and we apologize in advance for any unintentional omissions. We would be pleased to insert the appropriate acknowledgements in any subsequent edition of this publication.